Calman's SAVOY sketchbook

A selection taken from Mel Calman's Savoy sketchbooks

Calman's Savoy Sketchbook

Published by Aztec Design
31 Artillery Road
Guildford Surrey GU1 4NW

Printed in England

ISBN 0 9524782 0 X

© Claire and Stephanie Calman 1994
Drawings selected by Claire Calman

Dedication

For the staff of The Savoy, who treated our father almost as if he were a real guest...

Claire and Stephanie Calman
November 1994

Introduction

Mel Calman was one of life's true celebrants. He had that rare ability to make the bad things better and the good things very good indeed.

Beneath an artfully maintained veneer of lugubriousness lurked a man of copious and infectious enthusiasms. His air of world-weariness was a defence against short-term, fashionable enthusiasm for which he had little time. In fact he was one of the least world-weary people I ever met. He was constantly noticing things: "I rather like that", I hear him saying. It might have applied to a picture or a piece of gossip or a cake he'd never tried before. In one case it was an entire office block which he tried to interest me in buying. His enthusiasms were of the best sort, deeply, gently and persistently held. They were never forced upon you, though Mel had a considerable skill in making attractive to others whatever he found attractive at the time.

Ever since I worked with him in 1965, when he was the first, and quite probably the last resident cartoonist to be employed on a TV current affairs programme, our paths crossed at constant if irregular intervals. Like characters in Anthony Powell's *Dance to the Music of Time* we found ourselves coming together in disparate places — an hotel in Southern Ireland, on the Corniche at Cannes, at odd literary festivals or film screenings and we would take up where we left off, as naturally as if we saw each other daily.

I associate Mel most closely with London. He enjoyed city life and was a resident of Soho long after the Fitzroy Bohemians had gone and long before the Groucho Club arrived. He had a fondness for street life and caf life and his droll, contemplative humour and busy mind made him a wonderful companion.

To a provincial boy like myself, twenty-odd years a Sheffielder, Mel was a metropolitan sophisticate. Not in a narrow, affluent, clubbish sense, but in his appetite for and knowledge of the life of the city at large. However brief our meetings, I always learned something from Mel and my enjoyment of London life was greatly enriched by him. I was delighted, therefore, to hear of his Savoy Sketchbook. Nothing will replace the chance encounters and idle chats over coffee or a glass of wine but this book absolutely catches the flavour of Mel's company.

The hotel itself is a perfect subject for him. He admired quality in craftmanship and workmanship. He was drawn to tradition, not in any fogeyish way but through a fascination and admiration for things that worked and lasted. He had good taste and a fresh, idiosyncratic eye. His observations of The Savoy at work show delight in the pleasure of seeing how things are done, whether the task be chopping carrots or folding sheets. His ear is as good as his eye. The book is full of characterful eavesdroppings. Under-chefs advise newcomers to hang on to their knives. "That s why you keep them in your pockets. May not be there tomorrow." The head waiter is determined in dealing with the "video man": "He's not getting a meal. No way, no way." A chambermaid reflects on tips: "The Japanese leave something every day - usually a pound under the pillow".

It's an affectionate, revealing, entertaining book, a celebration of a great institution and a reminder of Mel Calman's humour, humanity and inimitable powers of observation.

Michael Palin

Foreword

Mel walked through the doors of The Savoy and fell in love. The atmosphere, the sense of excitement and, above all, the people, aroused his curiosity and delighted his artist's eye.
I know exactly how he felt. Like a hotelier, Mel was everywhere, looking closely at everything and everyone. And, like a good hotelier, he had a passionate eye for detail.

    It was a pleasure to know Mel. He was an amazing man with a terrific sense of humour and a personality of immense charm and charisma. I was totally taken aback to hear of his death, as I had seen him only a few hours before when he came here to talk about this book.

    For me, these drawings capture the magic of The Savoy. And, more importantly, they express Mel's unique wit, talent and humanity.

We all miss him.

Herbert Striessnig
Director and General Manager
The Savoy

Breakfast

I got a very positive response

croissants

What time scale are we talking?

Service table

Commis

One of the best equity funds —

Respectful

I've never seen him in a SUIT —
I've never seen him even in a tie — yet
here he is making 120% return in equity...

Grill room

Wine Waiter Tony →

Buzz of conversation – mostly male.

A rare sight – woman eating →

Hooks for orders
Service Station
commis
with long white apron

Mostly MEN -
only 2 women

afternoon tea 3 - 5·30 with musical accompaniment
180 - 200 people
on a Saturday afternoon

Should I have another cake?

WARM scones

Choices choices

It's mostly women
husbands wives - did their shopping
& now filling up on scones & cakes & tea
& more cakes...

Wasn't you fall?
in a play by Mel Calman?

American BAR

our love is here to stay as Time goes by

Dinner & Dancing SAT night

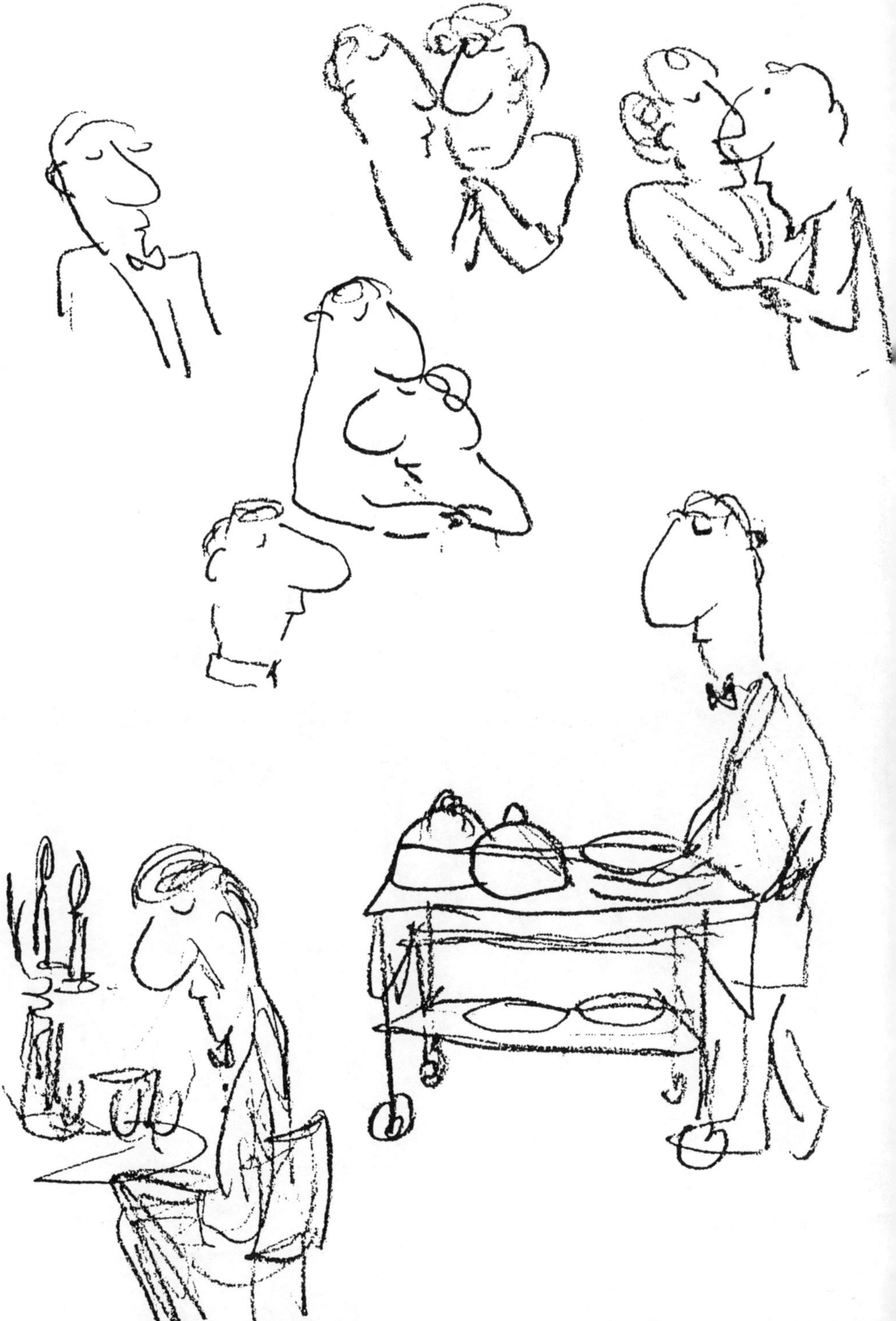

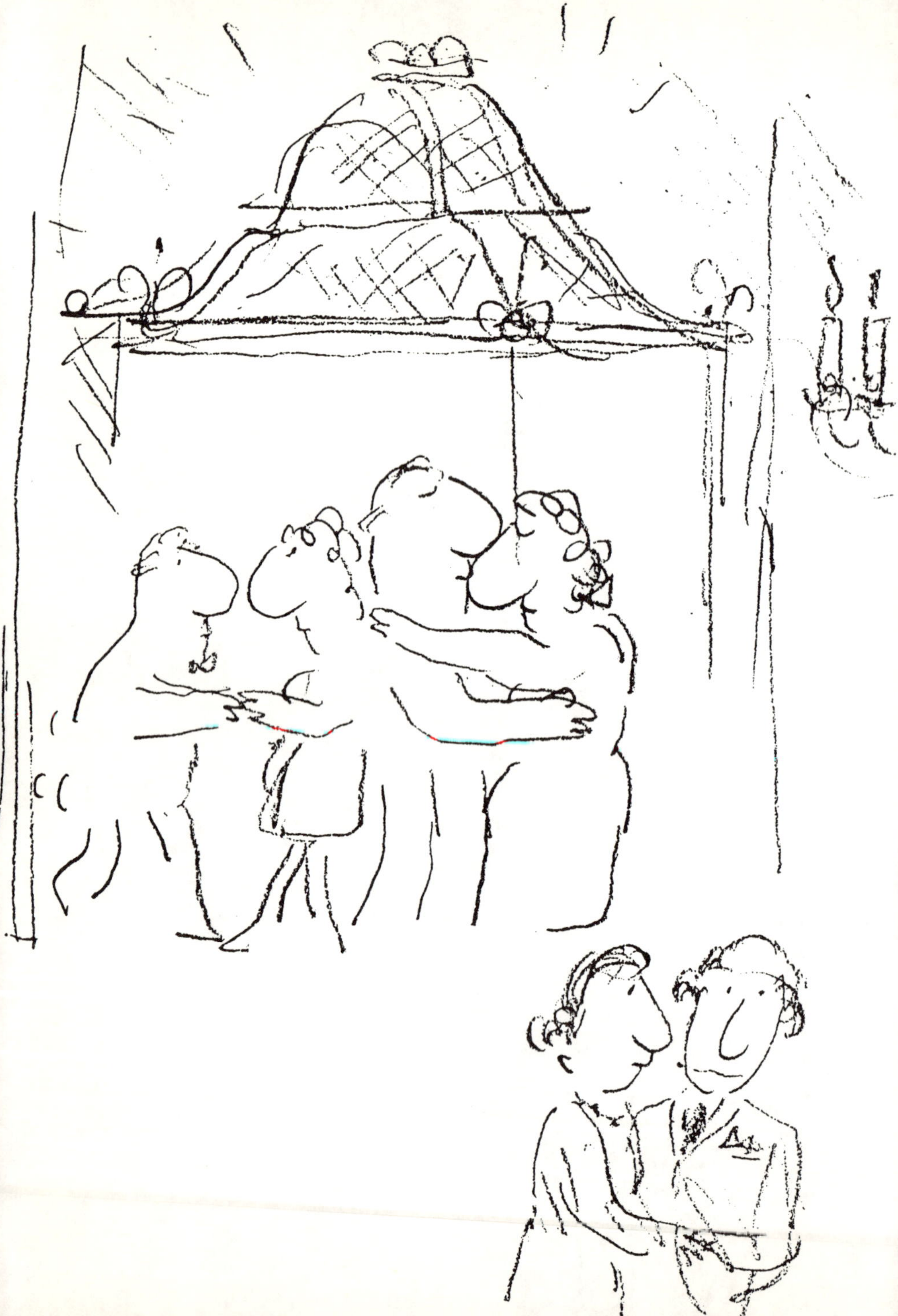

Champagne Gala Dinner

Seating plans

Sparkling

I can't come —
I shall be in
the Pyrenees

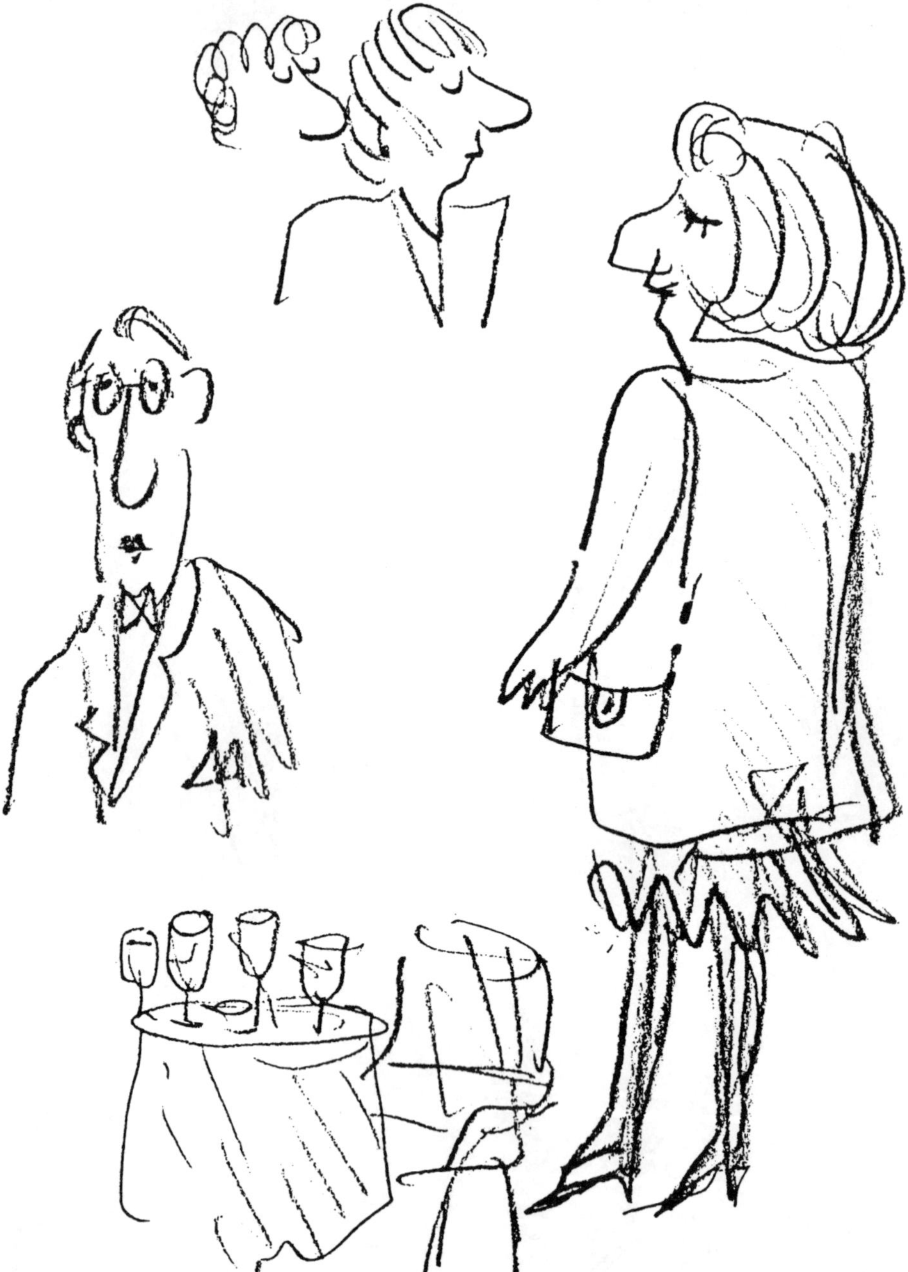

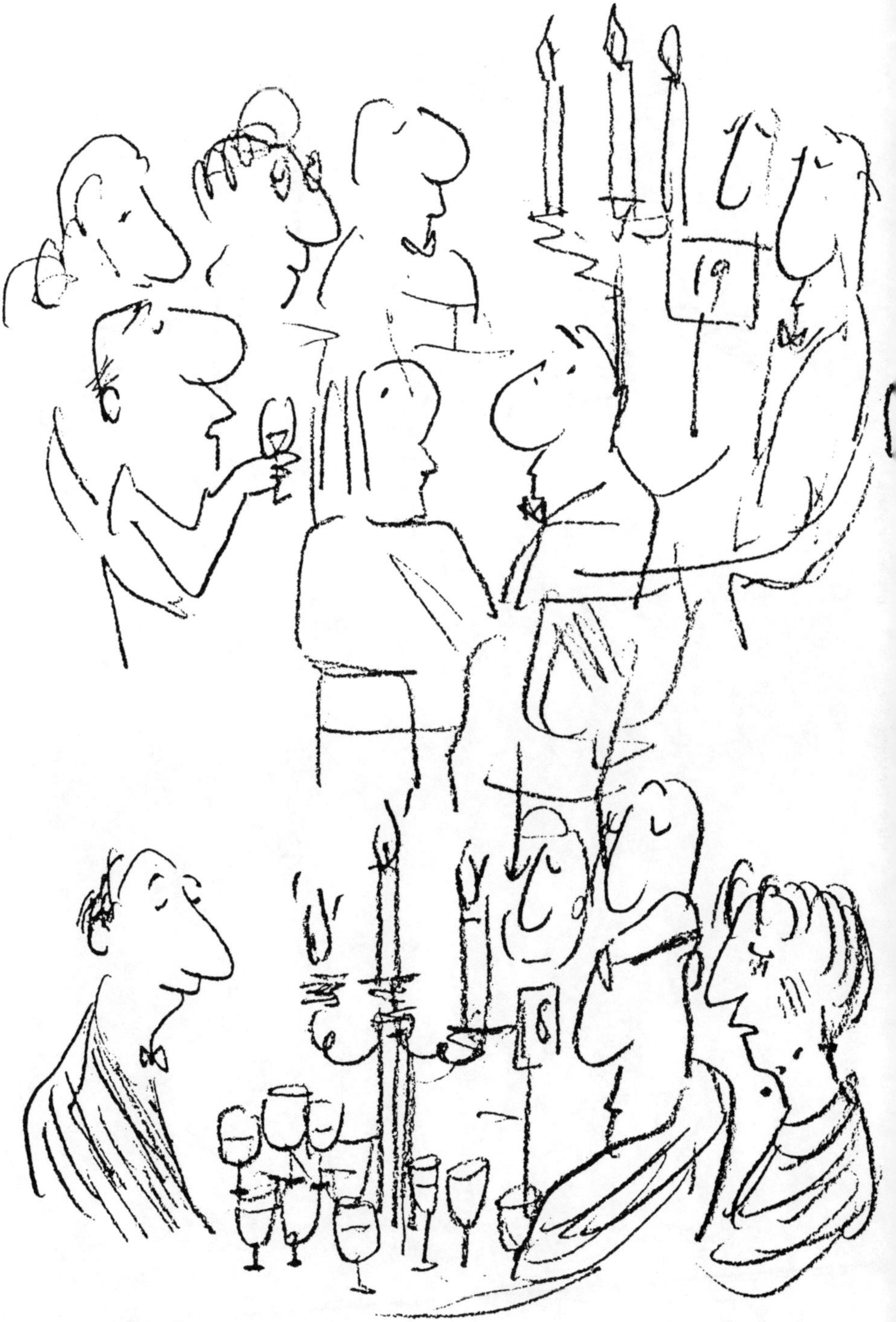

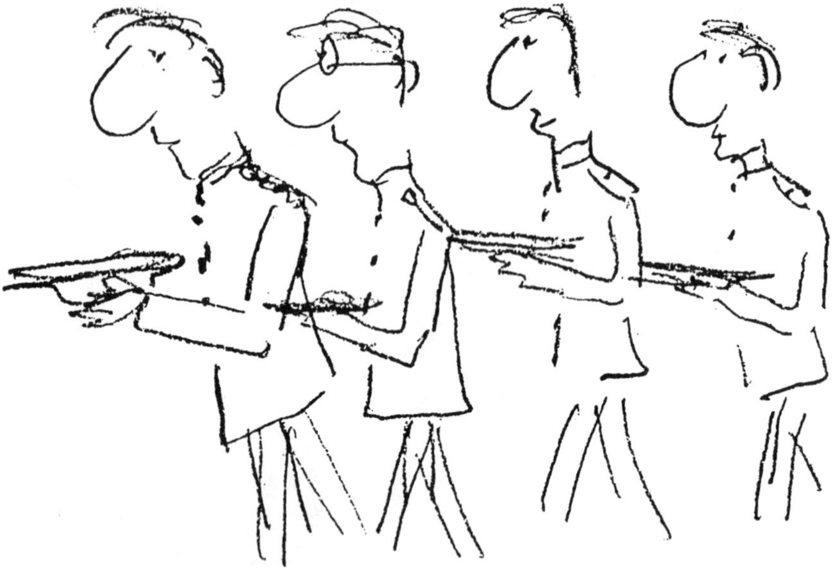

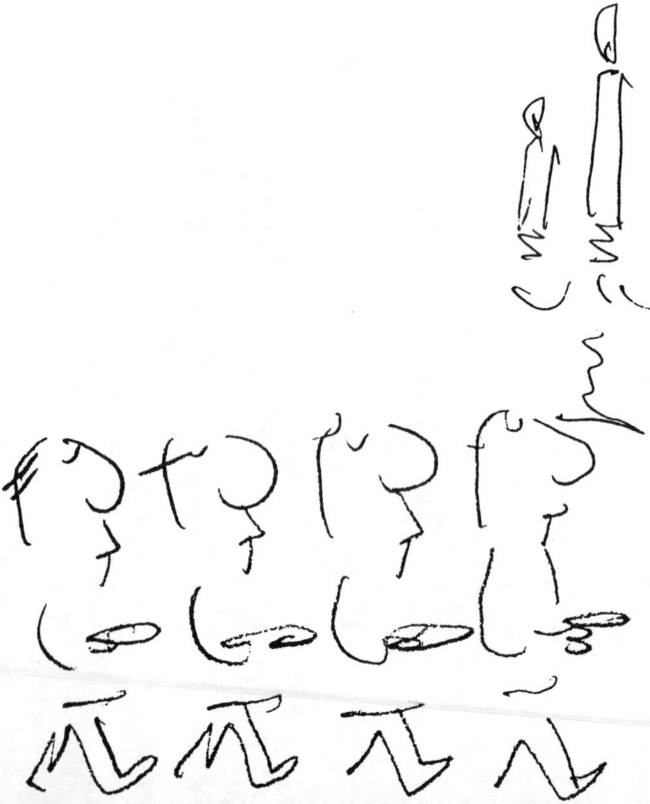

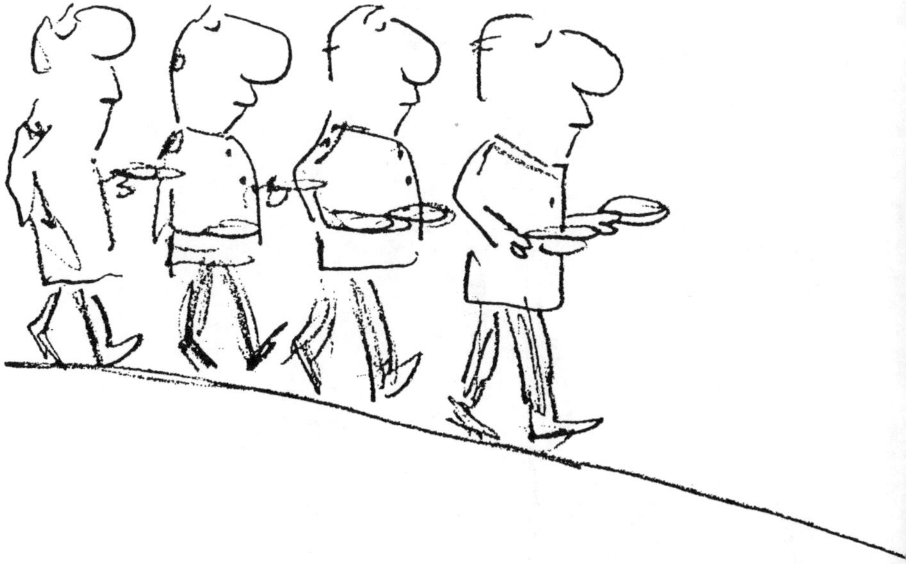

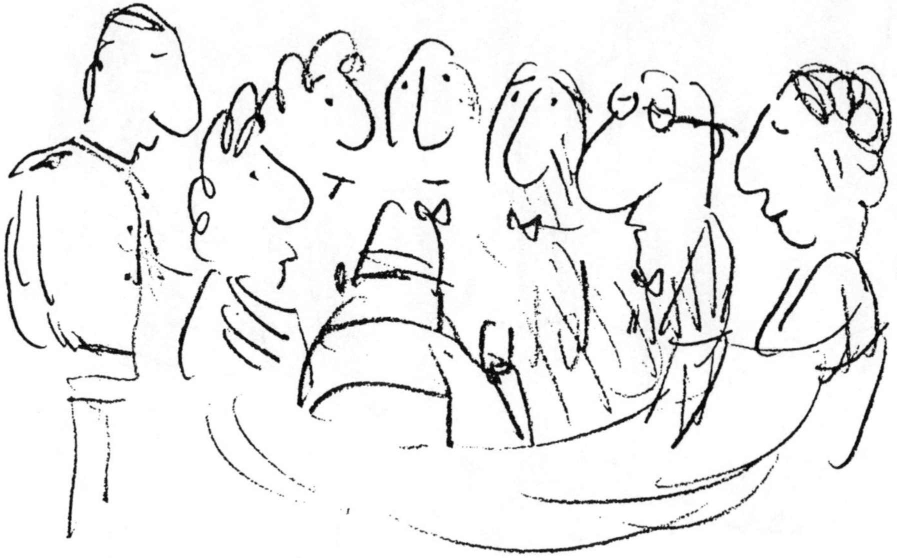

Toasting the President

There used to be 3 trumpets. Now there's only 2 — it's the recession

3 plates each · white gloves white jacket · THE ENTRY of the WAITERS · two more melons!

'Pellegrinos' — nickname for Italian waiters

Head waiter —
Can we get on with it ?
we'll be here till 1·30
as it is —

Head waiter-
He's Zefferelli
(scornful)
(about the
video man)
He's not getting
a meal-)
no way-
no way-!

BANQUETING. 7pm   Lodge Dinner Ladies
Lancaster   Waiting to sit down   Festival
Room

Meanwhile →
Behind the swing doors

80 - 90 Chefs

10:30 am

Tasting

Two tea towels from waist

Check trous

Chef breaking eggs

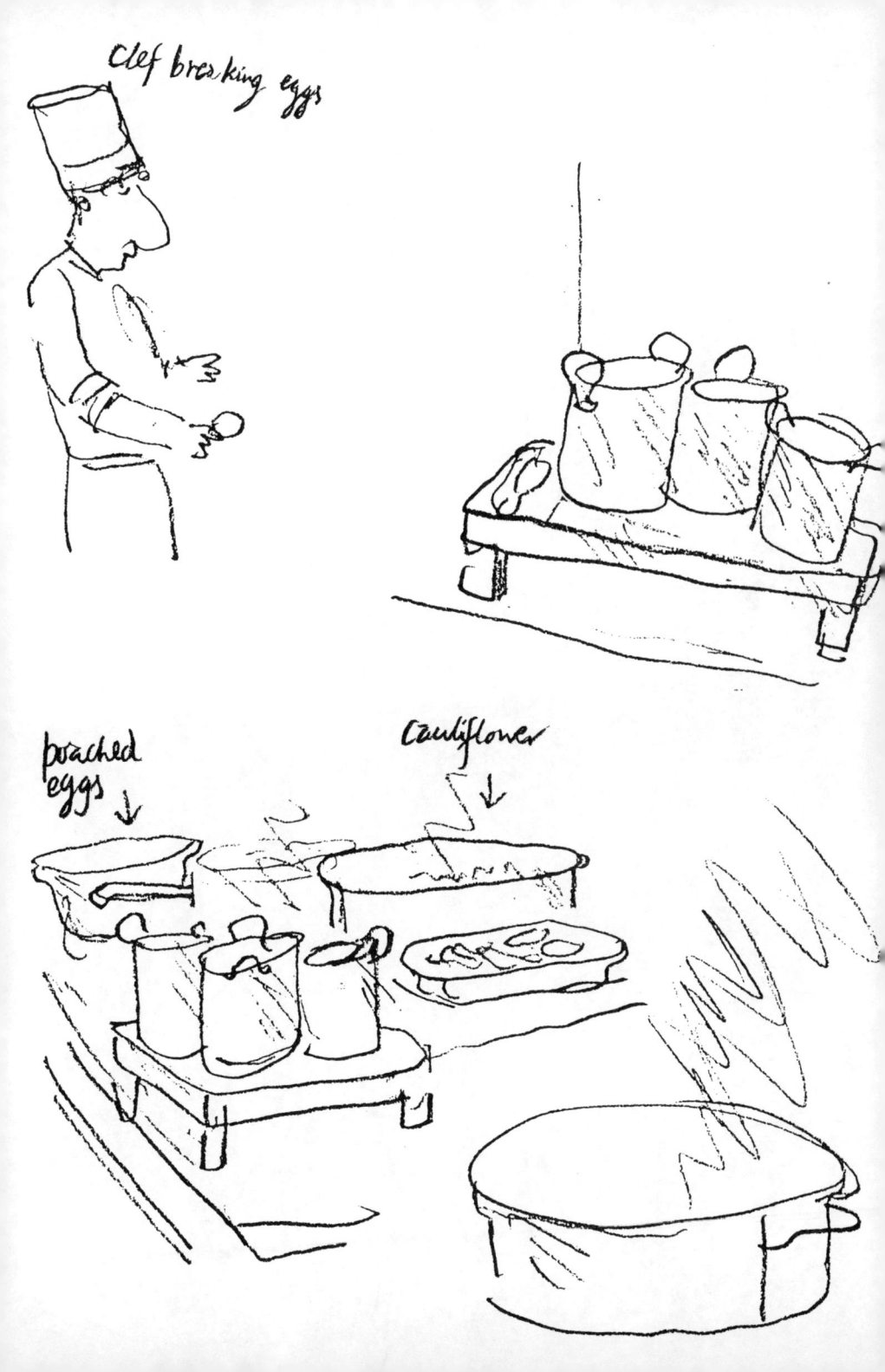

poached eggs ↓   cauliflower ↓

11am

wrapping courgette flowers

sliced ribbons of carrots

two cloths on waist

White snoods ↓

SHAVING ASparagus

Veg dish
mash
+ veg
rolled up
in flour
covered in 8twirls
deep fried
for 2 mins
with tomato
sauce

Bean bits

Flour

11·30
VEG

Plates

← Bags of onions

onions ↓

orders for food

Making croutons
Slicing bread

What I notice

Noise
BANGING of LIDS
PANS
Hustle/bustle/speed.
Quantities
So much of everything.
Peely bag of onions.
Poaching boxes of eggs
(it's like Buster Keaton
  in the Navigator)
Huge pans & frying pans

CHOPPING - MIXING -

Everything in piles/Rows/
Everyone absorbed, concentrated - speed
No waste of effort

Shredding
Cabbage

11·30

Heap of green
& yellow
Cabbage

"Keep your own
knives — it's
very hard —
that's why you
keep them in
your pockets.
May not be yours
tomorrow —

Trimming
Cabbages

Palette
smoothing
mash

Asparagus

(Noon)

BREAD Dept
Slicing – Making Melba toast

MARINO

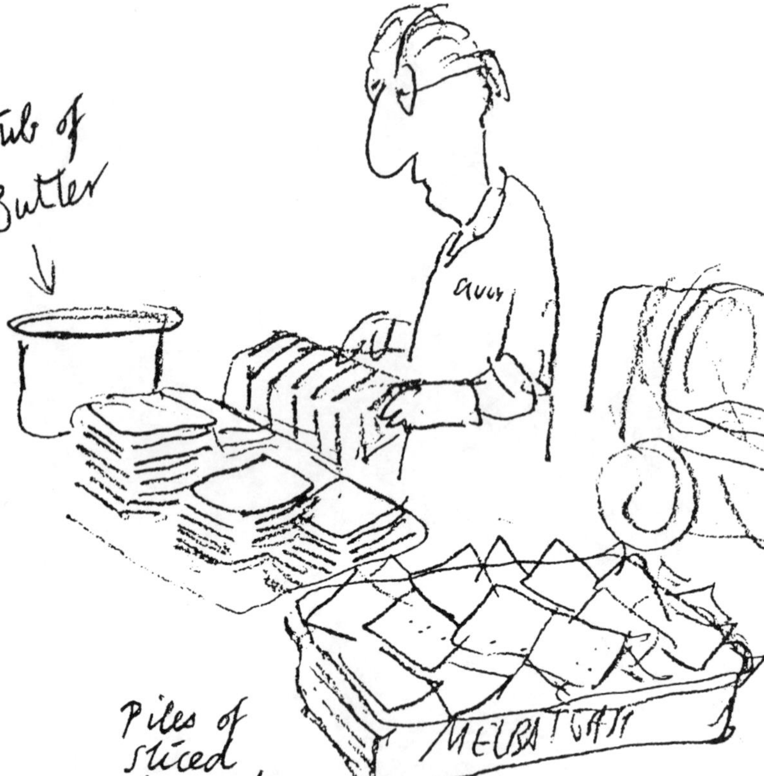

Prodding
Tasting
Shouting
Calling out
12·15
Things are hotting up
Potatoes
The chefs - commis quickstep

GOLD
& WHITE
Jackets
Black
trousers

8 gold
Buttons

Salad ↓

Edelmann goes around
tasting - checking -
criticizing - even
praising -

12.15 pm

Men
cleaning floors
constantly to mop up
debris etc

Ponytail

Dirty water

yellow
Bucket
on wheels

12.30
WAITERS ARRIVE
start to collect dishes

GOLD
frogging

putting
crisps
onto a
plate +
pink
napkins

WAITING for the orders.

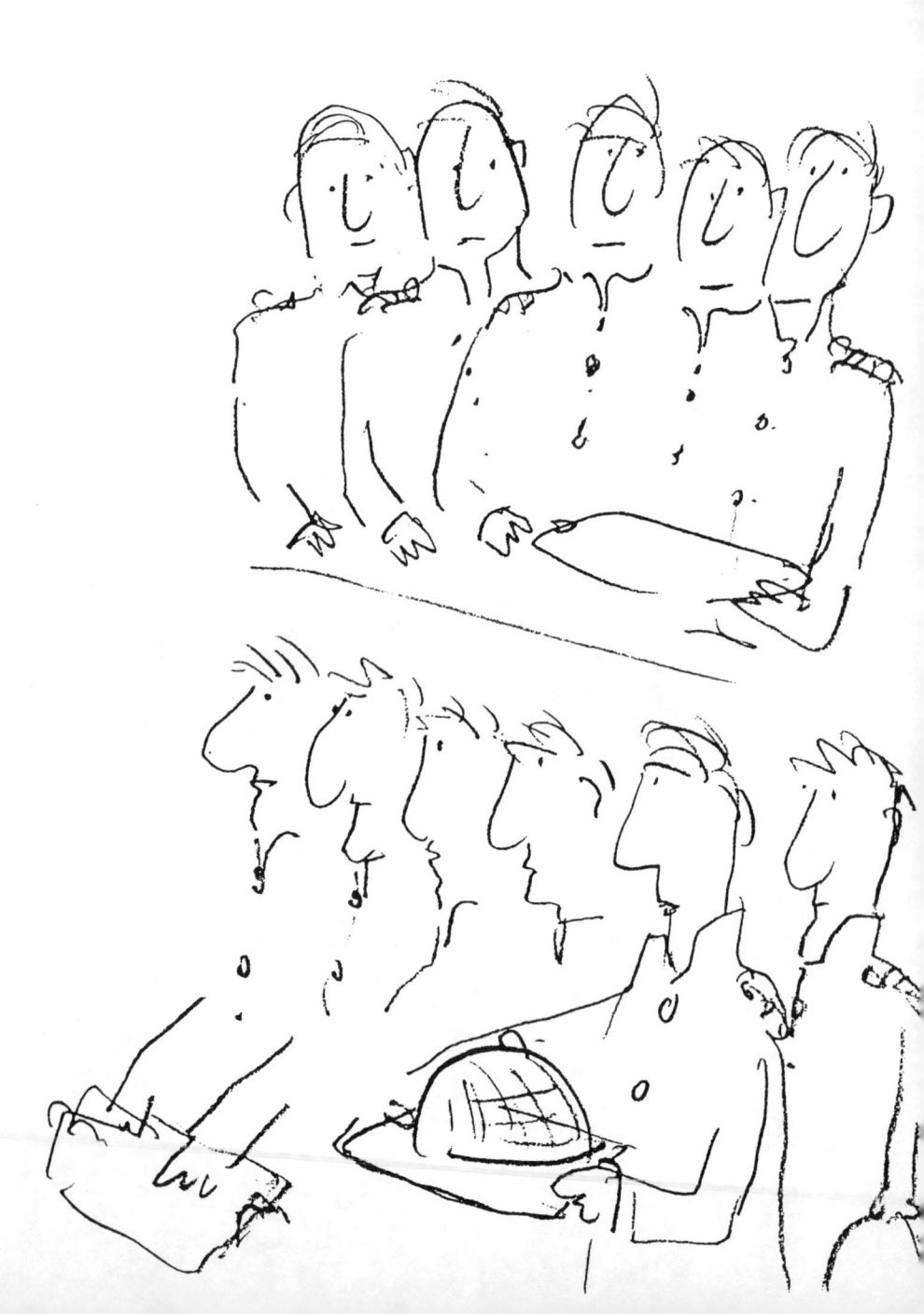

Preparing cheese trolley

grapes
apples
Fruit Basket

Pieces in foil
Cheese is unwrapped
then dipped in small bowl of water
to restore its freshness...

12·50

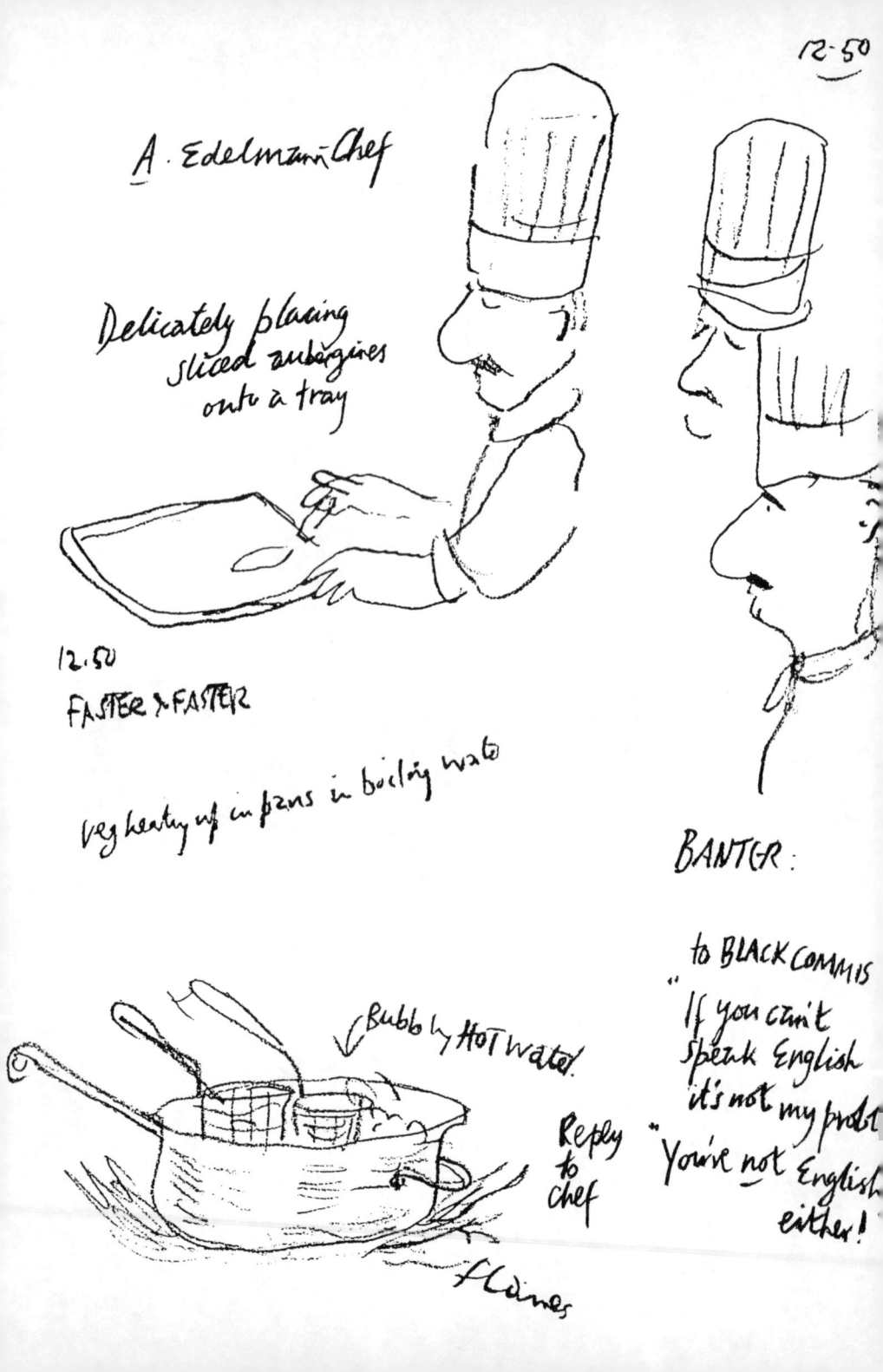

A. Edelman—Chef

Delicately placing
sliced aubergines
onto a tray

12.50
FASTER & FASTER

Veg heating up in pans in boiling water

Bubbly HOT water
Reply to chef
flames

BANTER:

to BLACK COMMIS
"If you can't speak English it's not my prob"
"You're not English either!"

Reaching
grabbing etc.

1.30
V. Busy LUNCH NOW

NOISE,
NOISE!
NOISE! BANGING
of
DISHES
, RUNNING!
SHOUTING! Plate,
ORDERS!

Waiting for the order to arrive

LAUNDRY & DRY cleaning - STAFF.
PINK - Restaurant. WHITE - Upstairs Bar & Banquets. BEIGE GRILL.

Shelves of LINEN

In the bowels of the Hotel. No natural light
Warm. the hum of machines
Good natured banter amongst the women & men —
One lady (Daphne) has been here 28 years.

3 - 4.00 - Busy at this time - waiters bringing their whites in to be cleaned/laundered

Lovely smell of fresh laundered linen

Blue striped dress

Personnel – TALK (Monday morning) to group of STAFF who have just joined SAVOY

Eric Beckey
Head of Personnel & Training
welcomes the Group – their first day.
" Feel at home – feel part of a family
over 600 members of STAFF –
it's large, it's old – it has a lot of
TRADITION – welcome to the SAVOY.
(33 NATIONALITIES in the HOTEL)

Valeting
5 in all
2 on each shift
7 – 1pm 1pm → 9pm
24 hours off

← Black ARM
Black lapel

Black TROUSERS

Departures - Check maintenance of Radio, TV.
Nothing left in drawer   Stripped - change linen etc

MAID 8 - till 4. 5-day week
" People tend not to leave tips. The Japanese leave something every day - usually £1 under the pillow."

Making the beds on the 6th floor

Flower Dept

A cold room in the
basement — tubs of flowers
on tables & on the floor

Colour! Colour! Colour!

Break at 9·30 for Tea or Nescafé

One girl lights up a cigarette
& two of them have a whisper and gossip in a corner.

Pale tulips ↓

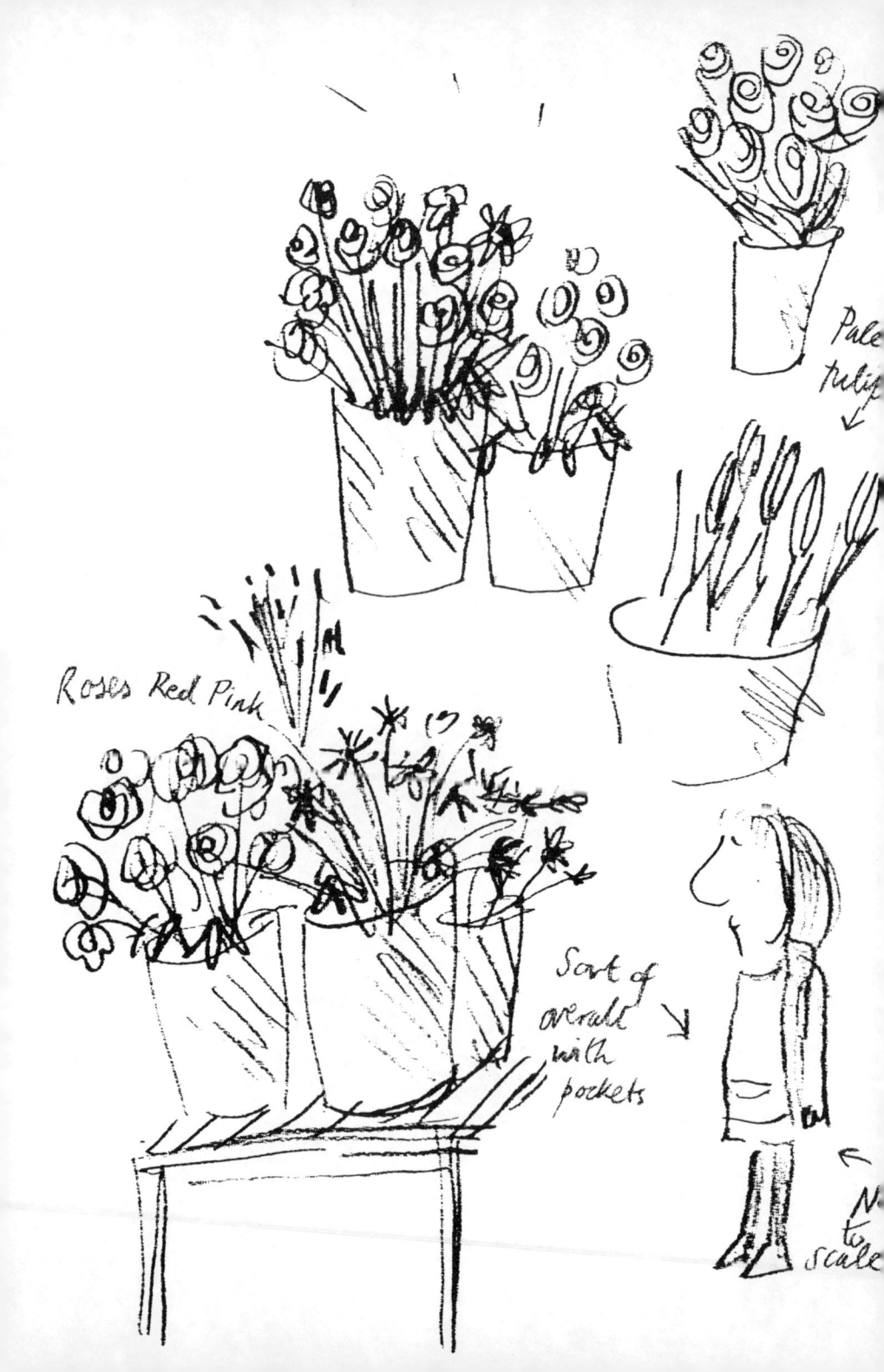

Roses Red Pink

Sort of overall with pockets →

← N to scale

'civilian clothes'
(ie not tails)

9.30
Meeting of Heads of
Dept.

(People leave
when no longer
needed)

ZANDER - Housekeeping

Housekeepers' meeting

10 Housekeepers in all

Dolly →

Notes from Head Housekeeper

"Honeymooners -
   Male & female slippers"

218 - Is that room ready?
530 Male slippers
234 - Female slippers

Notes on arrivals &
    departures -
Problems (There's a leak
    in 710)
All making notes on
    clipboards

Housekeepers' meeting 10.50 a.m.

One client comes every year. Whole floor — Brings his own furniture!

Art deco clock & chewing gum remover side by side

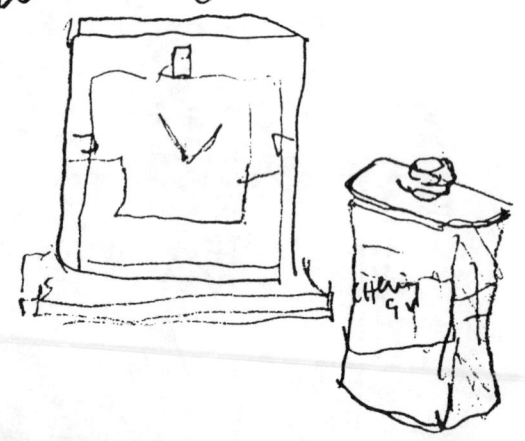

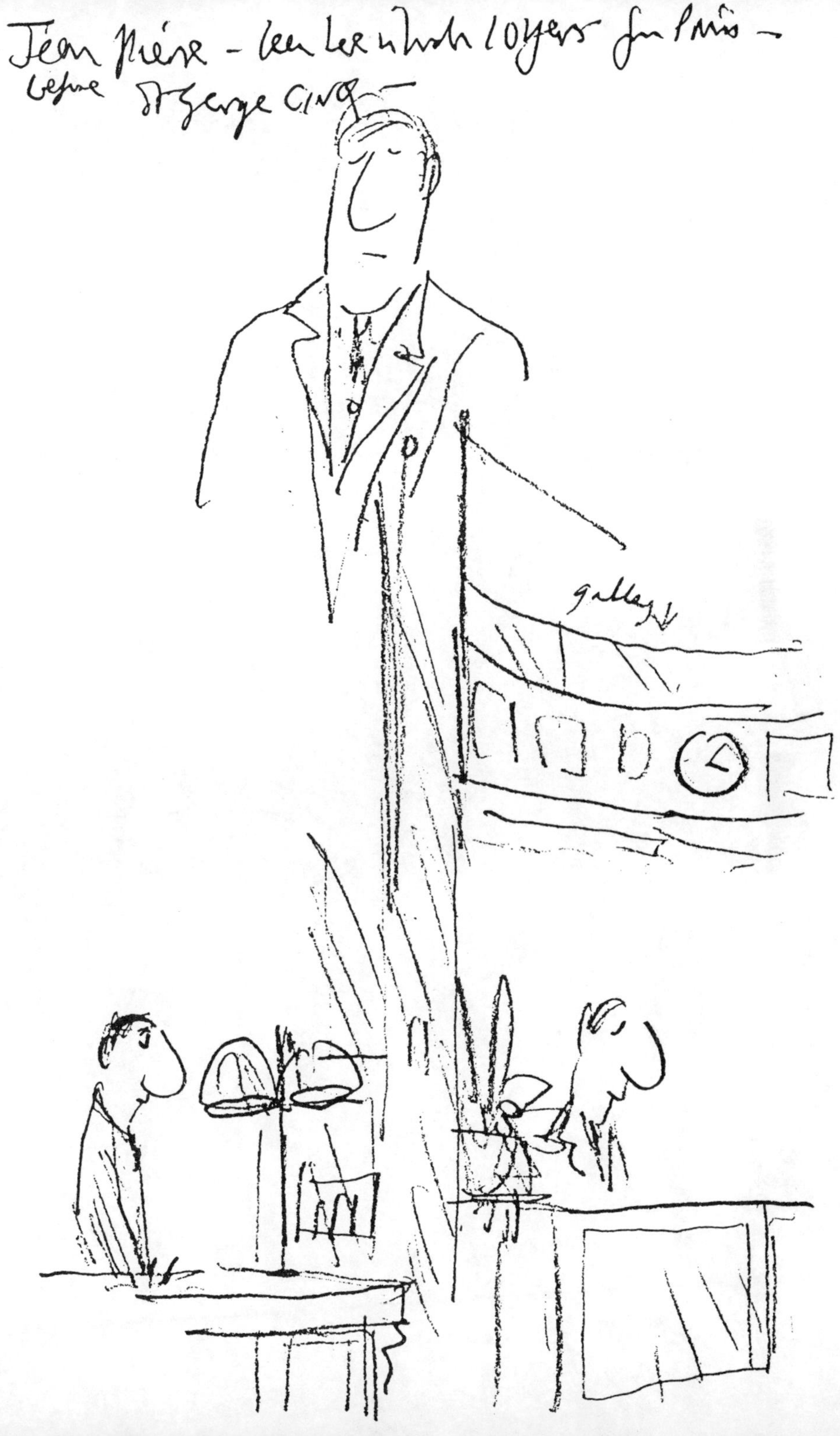
Jean Pierre –
10 years
Paris –
before St George Cinq –
gallery

Pigeonholes
Grey
Tail coat
Large silver
buttons
Jean Pierre
(not a
likeness)
Concierge desk